Profiles of the Presidents

WILLIAM HENRY HARRISON

★ ★ ★

Profiles of the Presidents

WILLIAM HENRY HARRISON

By Robin Doak

Content Adviser: Jason E. Poe, Historical Adviser, Berkeley Hundred Plantation, Charles City, Virginia

Reading Adviser: Dr. Linda D. Labbo, Department of Reading Education, College of Education, The University of Georgia

COMPASS POINT BOOKS ✦ MINNEAPOLIS, MINNESOTA

Compass Point Books
3109 West 50th Street, #115
Minneapolis, MN 55410

Visit Compass Point Books on the Internet at *www.compasspointbooks.com*
or e-mail your request to *custserv@compasspointbooks.com*

Photographs ©: White House Collection, Courtesy White House Historical Association (60), cover, 3;
National Portrait Gallery, Smithsonian Institution/Art Resource, N. Y., 6; Hulton/Archive by Getty
Images, 7, 12, 14, 19, 25 (bottom), 26, 32, 54 (right), 55 (top left & right), 56 (right, all), 58 (top
right); North Wind Picture Archives, 8, 9, 11, 15 (inset), 18, 20, 22, 23, 27, 28, 31, 35 (bottom), 36,
38, 55 (bottom left), 56 (bottom left); Dave G. Hauser/Corbis, 10, 54 (left); Library of Congress, 13,
15, 24, 33, 35 (top), 43, 48, 49, 57 (left), 59 (left); Ohio Historical Society, 16, 56 (top left); James P.
Rowan, 17; Stock Montage, 21, 30, 37; Collection of the Ross County Historical Society, 25 (top);
Lombard Antiquarian Maps & Prints, 29; Courtesy Martin Van Buren National Historical Park,
Kinderhook, New York, 40, 58 (left); U.S. Department of the Treasury, 42; Bettmann/Corbis, 45, 47;
Naval Historical Center, 46; Courtesy of the President Benjamin Harrison Home, Indianapolis, IN, 50;
Department of Rare Books and Special Collections, University of Rochester Library, 57 (bottom right);
Texas State Library & Archives Commission, 58 (bottom right); Bruce Burkhardt/Corbis, 59 (right).

Editors: E. Russell Primm, Emily J. Dolbear, Melissa McDaniel, and Catherine Neitge
Photo Researcher: Svetlana Zhurkina
Photo Selector: Linda S. Koutris
Designer/Page Production: The Design Lab/Les Tranby
Cartographer: XNR Productions, Inc.

Library of Congress Cataloging-in-Publication Data
Doak, Robin S. (Robin Santos), 1963–
    William Henry Harrison / by Robin Doak.
      p. cm. — (Profiles of the presidents)
Summary: A biography of the ninth president of the United States, discussing his
personal life, education, and political career.
Includes bibliographical references (p.) and index.
    ISBN 0-7565-0257-8 (alk. paper)
    1. Harrison, William Henry, 1773–1841—Juvenile literature. 2. Presidents—United States—
Biography—Juvenile literature. [1. Harrison, William Henry, 1773–1841. 2. Presidents.] I. Title. II. Series.
    E392 .D625 2003
    973.5'8'092—dc21   2002153564

Table of Contents

★ ★ ★

NOTE: In this book, words that are defined in the glossary are
in **bold** the first time they appear in the text.

Old Tippecanoe

★ ★ ★

William Henry Harrison, military hero and ninth president of the United States

No one knows what kind of president William Henry Harrison would have been. Harrison, the nation's ninth president, spent just one month in office. No president has ever served a shorter term. As a result, historians can only guess what Harrison would have done if he had served a full four-year term.

Harrison didn't have a chance to prove himself as president. However, he did have a long and successful career as a U.S. Army officer and a public official. In the army, he earned fame around the nation as an "Indian fighter" who defeated Native Americans trying to hold on to their lands. A battle

at the Tippecanoe River in
Indiana in 1811 earned him
the nickname that stuck with
him for the rest of his life—
Old Tippecanoe.

Harrison was also the
first governor of the Indiana
Territory. He worked tirelessly
to convince white settlers to
come to the region. Harrison
also arranged treaties, or agree-
ments between two governments,
with nearby Native American
tribes. These treaties gave the
United States millions of acres of
land in Indiana, Illinois, Wisconsin, and Michigan.

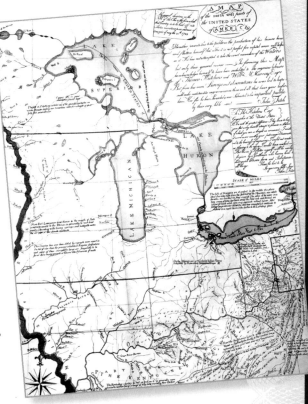

▲ A 1785 map showing
the Great Lakes and
the area that would
one day be divided
into the states of
Illinois, Indiana,
Michigan, Ohio,
and Wisconsin

Harrison's short term as president had one important
effect: His death forced Congress and the nation to exam-
ine the way power is transferred from the president to the
vice president. It also encouraged Americans to look more
closely at the person running for vice president. There is
no way to know whether that individual will suddenly
have to take over if something happens to the president.

Young Harrison

★ ★ ★

Benjamin Harrison ▼ played an important role in the Revolutionary War.

On February 9, 1773, the Harrison family of Charles City County, Virginia, welcomed their seventh and final child into the world. William Henry Harrison was born into a wealthy family. His mother, Elizabeth Bassett Harrison, came from an old and well-respected Virginia family. William's father, Benjamin, was a close friend of George Washington, who would one day become the first president of the United States.

Much of William's childhood was colored by the Revolutionary War (1775–1783), which began when he was just two years old. His father played an important role in the struggle for independence from Great Britain and the birth of the new nation. He signed the Declaration of Independence and was also present at the First and Second Continental Congresses. The congresses led the nation as it was breaking away from Britain. Benjamin Harrison later served three terms as governor of Virginia.

Despite his family's fortune, William knew he would have to make his own way in the world. At that time, a family's land usually went to the oldest son, and he was the youngest of seven children. When William was a teenager, he attended Hampden-Sydney College in Virginia for a short time. He then moved to Richmond, Virginia, to live with one of his brothers.

▲ *The signers of the Declaration of Independence, including Benjamin Harrison, who is second from the left near the bottom in the yellow coat*

In Richmond, William began studying medicine. To further his education, he traveled to Philadelphia, Pennsylvania, in 1790. There he intended to study under Dr. Benjamin Rush, who was a friend of his father.

However, William's father died the following year. Benjamin Harrison's youngest child was left with little money. By that time, though, he had decided that a career in medicine was not for him. He wanted a life of fighting and adventure. At the age of eighteen, he joined the U.S. Army.

William Henry ▼ Harrison was born on Berkeley Plantation in Charles City County, Virginia.

Army Officer and Governor

★ ★ ★

As a young army officer, Harrison was sent to Fort Washington in the Northwest Territory. The Northwest Territory included what is now Ohio, Indiana,

▾ *Fort Washington, near Cincinnati, Ohio, was built in 1789.*

Michigan, Illinois, and part of Minnesota. The U.S. government was encouraging people to move there because it wanted to control the territory. As more settlers moved into the region, however, problems arose. The Native Americans who had lived there for many years resented the newcomers. Fort Washington, near present-day Cincinnati, Ohio, served as a barrier between the white settlers and the Native Americans.

General Anthony Wayne commanded Harrison at the Battle of Fallen Timbers.

Tensions between the two groups came to a head in 1794 at the Battle of Fallen Timbers. This battle between Native Americans and U.S. Army troops at Fort Washington marked the end of Native American fighting in the Ohio region. It opened up the area for settlement by white Americans.

The Battle of Fallen Timbers was Harrison's first battle. It gave him a chance to prove his worth, and he fought bravely. Harrison's commander, General Anthony Wayne, noted the young officer's courage.

The following year, General Wayne died and Harrison was given command of Fort Washington. Later in the year, Harrison married twenty-year-old Anna Tuthill Symmes. Anna had grown up in New York and New Jersey and was both educated and beautiful. She and her father, a judge, had recently arrived at Fort Washington. Anna's father was against the marriage, but the young couple snuck away and got married anyway.

▲ *Anna Tuthill Symmes married William Henry Harrison in 1795.*

Benjamin Harrison, ▶
the grandson of
William Henry
Harrison, was
elected president
in 1888.

Anna would prove to be a loyal and patient army wife, following her husband from one post to another. Over the years, the Harrisons had ten children. Sadly, only four of them lived long enough to see their father achieve the highest office in the land, and just two would live past the age of forty. One of Harrison's grandsons would one day follow in his grandfather's footsteps. In 1888, Benjamin Harrison would be elected the twenty-third president of the United States.

◂ President John Adams appointed Harrison secretary of the Northwest Territory.

◂ Members of Congress met at Federal Hall in New York City

In 1798, Harrison decided to leave the army. Soon, President John Adams named him secretary of the Northwest Territory. Two years later, Harrison was elected the territory's first delegate, or representative, to the U.S. Congress. In Congress, Harrison backed the Land Act of 1800, which made it easier for settlers to buy government lands in the Northwest Territory.

★

William Henry ▶
Harrison as
governor of the
Indiana Territory

In 1800, President Adams appointed Harrison the first governor of the newly created Indiana Territory. This included all or part of what is now Indiana, Illinois, Michigan, Minnesota, and Wisconsin. The young politician was handsome and likable, and his star was on the rise.

Harrison moved to the territory's capital, present-day Vincennes, Indiana. He built a huge home, which he named Grouseland. During nine of Harrison's twelve years as governor, Grouseland was both the social and official center of the territory.

As governor, Harrison's job was to oversee Native American affairs. He had to make sure that Native Americans were treated well by white settlers. Harrison ordered that they be given medicine to protect them from smallpox, a deadly disease brought to the territory by the settlers. He tried to do his best for them.

◄ *Grouseland is located in Vincennes, Indiana.*

However, Harrison also had another reponsibility as governor, and this duty caused much conflict and bloodshed in the region. He was to buy as much land as possible from the Native Americans for the U.S. government. Over the years, Harrison worked out a number of treaties in which native tribes exchanged millions of acres of land for relatively little money. Most Native Americans did not understand the idea of land ownership. They did not believe people could own the land any more than they could own the air. As a result, the tribes signed over the rights to their lands. If a tribe didn't want to sign away their land, Harrison gave their chiefs alcohol to muddle their thinking.

U.S. troops destroyed a Native American village. As Harrison worked to buy more Native American lands, there was increased conflict in the area he governed.

Eventually, the governor got the tribes to sign over about 60 million acres (24 million hectares) of land to the United States. One of the most famous of these "land grabs" was the Treaty of Fort Wayne. In this treaty, the United States got 3 million acres (1 million hectares) of land. The tribes that signed the treaty got as little as $200 each year in exchange.

The Treaty of Fort Wayne was the final straw for one Native American chief. Tecumseh, a leader of the Shawnee tribe, decided that the time had come to rise up against the U.S. government. He began to organize Native American tribes to take back their land. Tecumseh also hoped to get help from the British, who still claimed parts of the Indiana Territory as their own.

▲ *Tecumseh was a Shawnee leader who organized several Native American tribes in an attempt to regain their land.*

Tecumseh and
William Henry
Harrison confront
each other at their
unsuccessful meeting
at Grouseland in
August 1810.

On August 15, 1810, Tecumseh and seventy-five warriors visited Grouseland to meet with the governor. The meeting was a complete failure. When Tecumseh left Grouseland, he was prepared for war. The chief traveled throughout the region, gathering support from other tribes. As more people joined him, he and his warriors began raiding American settlements.

Tenskwatawa, who was known as the Prophet, was Tecumseh's half-brother.

In early November 1811, Harrison set out to punish Tecumseh for the raids. The governor and about a thousand men marched toward a settlement of warriors headed by Tenskwatawa, who was Tecumseh's half-brother. The Native American warriors were camped along the Tippecanoe River in northern Indiana. Tecumseh was away, trying to gather support for his cause.

On the night of November 6, the Native Americans attacked Harrison's men. Tenskwatawa, who was also called the Prophet, had promised his men that they could not be harmed by the white men's bullets. He was wrong. Harrison's men defeated the Prophet's forces. Any warriors who survived the battle fled. Tecumseh's dream was destroyed.

News of Harrison's victory at the Battle of Tippecanoe traveled across the nation. Harrison had triumphed at another major battle. His fame as a great warrior and leader continued to grow.

William Henry ▶
Harrison's troops
defeated Native
American forces
at the Battle of
Tippecanoe in 1811.

War Hero and Politician

★   ★   ★

In June 1812, the United States and Great Britain again found themselves at war with one another. The two countries disagreed over territory in the West. During the War of 1812 (1812–1814), many Native Americans fought on the side of the British. Tecumseh and his followers were among those who took up arms against the United States.

At the beginning of the war, Harrison was made a brigadier general. A few months later, he was promoted

◀ *The USS Constitution being chased by British ships during the War of 1812*

to major general and put in command of the entire Army of the Northwest. By the end of September 1813, Harrison had helped recapture Detroit, Michigan, which had fallen earlier into enemy hands.

On October 5, Harrison added even more fame and glory to his name. During the Battle of the Thames, in Ontario, Canada, Harrison and more than 5,000 men fought against a British and Native American force of 1,700 men. The Americans easily won. During this battle, Tecumseh was killed. It was also the final battle of the war in the Northwest.

Tecumseh was killed during the Battle of the Thames.

Harrison was now famous. He asked to take a break from the army and traveled through New York, Pennsylvania, and Washington, D.C. He was greeted by adoring crowds everywhere he went. In May 1814, Harrison left the army for good and retired to his farm near Cincinnati, Ohio.

However, Harrison found it difficult to make ends meet as a farmer. He and his family spent more than they earned. Soon, Harrison was in debt and turned to politics to support his family.

▼ This letter written to Harrison in 1814 by three soldiers who were under his command praises his military leadership.

◄ The Harrison farm near Cincinnati, Ohio

John Quincy Adams ▶
appointed Harrison
minister to Colombia.

In 1816, Harrison won his first elected position and became a U.S. congressman from Ohio. He served one term in Washington before winning a seat as an Ohio state senator. He held this spot for two years. In 1825, Harrison returned to Washington, this time as a U.S. senator from Ohio. He held this job until 1828, when President John Quincy Adams appointed him **minister** to Colombia.

◄ *Andrew Jackson became the seventh president of the United States in 1829.*

In March 1829, Andrew Jackson became the new president of the United States. Harrison hoped that Jackson would give him another government job, but he was disappointed. Instead, Harrison came home from Colombia and spent the next eight years working on his farm in North Bend. Again, the Harrisons had money problems. He was eventually forced to take a low-paying job as a court clerk to earn a living.

Tippecanoe and Tyler Too

★ ★ ★

Harrison's fortunes changed in 1836. That year, the Whig Party decided to try a new approach to defeat the Democrats and win the White House. They chose three **candidates** to run for president, and each was from a different part of the country. From the Northeast, the Whigs chose Daniel Webster of Massachusetts. Hugh Lawson White of Tennessee was chosen to appeal to Southern voters. To gain votes in the Northwest, the party chose William Henry Harrison of Ohio. The Whig Party hoped that the three candidates would be able to steal enough votes from the Democratic candidate, Martin Van Buren, to keep him from winning. Van Buren's chances were good, however, because he was close to the

Daniel Webster was one of the three Whig candidates in the 1836 presidential election.

popular president, Andrew Jackson. Still, if the Whigs could get enough votes to keep Van Buren from getting a majority, then the election would be sent to the House of Representatives. The House would then decide the winner. The Whigs believed that they had a good chance of making a deal in the House that would get a Whig elected president.

However, not everyone thought this was a good **strategy** for winning. An editor of a Democratic newspaper called the *Richmond Enquirer* noted, "They have 'too many cooks'—and their broth may be spoiled."

The Whig strategy failed, although not by much. Van Buren received just over half of the popular vote and 170 electoral votes. William Henry Harrison came in second.

▼ *Martin Van Buren won the 1836 presidential election.*

Shortly after Van Buren's election, the nation faced a terrible economic **depression.** Hundreds of banks closed. Businesses failed, and many people lost their jobs. Some Americans also lost their homes and were forced into the streets. In New York City, hungry citizens rioted for food. Support for President Van Buren quickly disappeared. Critics painted him as a rich, uncaring snob.

An illustration from ▼ a pro-Harrison pamphlet criticizing Martin Van Buren

VAN BUREN AND RUIN.

Because of the economic depression, the Whigs knew that they had a good chance of winning the next presidential election. First, though, they had to choose the right candidate. Both of the top Whig leaders, Henry Clay of Kentucky and Daniel Webster of Massachusetts, believed they should be nominated. However, it quickly became clear that neither man had enough popular support to win.

▲ Henry Clay was angry that he was not nominated as the Whig presidential candidate in the 1840 election.

The Whigs soon turned to Harrison. He had been the most promising Whig candidate in the last election. He also had been out of the public eye for a while, so he wasn't tied to any issues that upset people. At the Whigs' national **convention** in December 1839, party members chose Harrison as their candidate over an angry and disappointed Henry Clay.

The Whigs chose ▶
John Tyler
for Harrison's
running mate.

For vice president, the Whigs selected John Tyler of Virginia. Tyler had much in common with his running mate. Both had been born in Charles City County, Virginia. Both came from wealthy, well-known families. Both held slaves, and both had served in the U.S. Congress.

The Whigs decided to try the same strategy that the Democrats had used to get Andrew Jackson elected to the

White House in 1828. During that **campaign,** the Democrats had focused on Jackson's war experience, proclaiming him a national hero. Early in the 1840 campaign, the Whigs began promoting Harrison's military career.

◄ An 1840 campaign banner shows scenes of Harrison's home, military career, and political activities.

The entire campaign focused more on style than political issues. At their convention, the Whigs had decided against adopting a party platform, which is a list of goals and ideals supported by the party. Instead, the Whigs wanted to make sure that Harrison did not take a stand on any issue that might lose him votes. His role in the campaign was to look like a great American war hero.

The Whigs stood behind their candidate. Even a disappointed Henry Clay supported Harrison. Party members began making speeches for him across the nation.

Some Democrats tried to make fun of Harrison for being a poor man from the country. One Democratic newspaper in Baltimore, Maryland, said that he should be given some hard cider, an alcoholic drink, and sent home to his log cabin. The Whigs took this image and used it to their advantage. They called Harrison's effort to be elected the "Log Cabin and Hard Cider" campaign. It became the nation's first modern campaign and served as a model for future presidential races.

Having recently suffered through a severe economic depression, the American people were looking for fun. The Whigs gave it to them. With the catchy **slogan** "Tippecanoe and Tyler Too," the Harrison-Tyler campaign

A campaign poster from 1840 showing Harrison offering hard cider to two soliders outside a log cabin

Campaigners for Harrison and Tyler push a tin ball in the event that gave Americans the slang phrase "keep the ball rolling."

quickly took on a circuslike atmosphere. The Whigs held parades, bonfires, and rallies for their candidates. At some events, they passed out hard cider, which an alcohol maker named E. G. Booz had given them. Another activity involved people pushing a 10-foot (3-meter) paper and tin ball for hundreds of miles. This campaign gave Americans the slang word *booze* for alcohol and the phrase "keep the ball rolling."

The cover of the Log Cabin Song Book used in Harrison's campaign

The Whigs portrayed Harrison as a man of the people. They encouraged the idea that he had been raised in a log cabin. Of course, nothing was further from the truth. The Whigs were also quick to remind the public of Martin Van Buren's problems as president. They nicknamed him Martin Van Ruin. In addition, they made up songs that were published in the *Log Cabin Song Book* and sung around the nation.

Harrison avoided taking stands on how he would handle the nation's problems. Most of the time, he just said that he would follow the will of Congress. Harrison, like many Whigs, believed that the people expressed their wishes through their locally elected leaders. Instead of talking about political issues, Harrison entertained the crowds by retelling war stories.

During the campaign, Harrison's health was a common topic. Even people in his own party worried about it. If he won, the sixty-seven year old would become the oldest president ever elected. Daniel Webster said, "If General Harrison lives, he will be president."

On the day of the election, 80 percent of all eligible voters turned out. It was one of the best voter turnouts in U.S. history. Harrison received only about 150,000 more votes than Van Buren, but he won easily in the electoral college. He defeated Van Buren 234 to 60.

▲ *William Henry Harrison was sixty-seven years old when he campaigned for president.*

Back to Washington

★ ★ ★

Washington, D.C., ▼
in the 1840s

William Henry Harrison arrived in Washington, D.C., on February 9, 1841, which was his sixty-eighth birthday. His wife, however, was not with him. Anna was not alto-

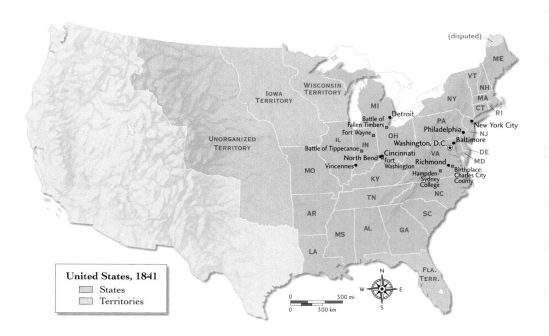

United States, 1841
- States
- Territories

gether happy about her husband's new job. When she received news of his victory, she said, "I wish that my husband's friends had left him where he is, happy and contented in retirement." Anna was also in poor health and was mourning the death of one of her children. For the first time since their marriage, she decided not to follow her husband. Instead, Anna stayed behind in Ohio to wait for warmer weather.

One of the first things Harrison did in Washington was to go to the White House and pay a visit to outgoing President Van Buren. In return, Van Buren visited Harrison and invited him to dine at the White House. After meeting Harrison, Van Buren said about him,

President Van Buren ▶
invited President-
elect Harrison
to dine at the
White House.

"He talks and thinks with much ease. . . . He is as tick-
led with the presidency as is a young woman with a
new bonnet."

Even before he took office, Harrison began to understand what it would be like to be president. No matter
where he went, he was surrounded by men seeking government jobs. Despite this, the friendly, easygoing Harrison
continued touring Washington without any aides. He
shook hands and talked with everyone he met. In the
evening, he was kept busy with dinners and parties.

Because Harrison was so easygoing, Whig congress-
men believed that they would be able to easily control
him. Senator Henry Clay of Kentucky was particularly
eager to take charge. He had wanted to be the Whig candidate for president. As a leader of the party—in the
Senate and elsewhere—he believed he deserved it. Now,
he was determined to control Harrison and run the government, even if he wasn't officially the nation's leader.

In Washington, Harrison soon heard the rumors
that he would be nothing more than Clay's **puppet**.
Clay did not deny these rumors. As a result, the two
men butted heads almost as soon as Harrison arrived
in the nation's capital.

*Thomas Ewing was ▶
Harrison's choice for
secretary of the
treasury, a decision
that upset Senator
Henry Clay.*

One of Harrison's tasks before being sworn in as president was to choose his **cabinet.** When the future president refused to give a job in the Treasury Department to the politician Clay wanted to see in that position, the Kentucky senator was furious. In a meeting with Harrison, Clay pushed his case. He tried to convince the future president to change his mind. Harrison finally lost his temper and said, "Mr. Clay, you forget that *I* am the president."

The Shortest Presidency

★   ★   ★

March 4, 1841, was a wet, cold, wintry day. Huge crowds gathered to greet the new president. Coatless, Harrison rode on horseback through the streets, waving his hat as he went.

◄ Crowds gathered in front of the White House for the inauguration of President Harrison.

Outside the Capitol, Harrison gave his inaugural address to a crowd of 50,000 people. In the speech, Harrison promised to uphold the **Constitution** and to follow the will of Congress. He said that it was wrong "to suppose that the president . . . could better understand the wants and wishes of the people than their own immediate representatives."

Harrison vowed to reform the way people were given government jobs. He said he would try to keep the peace among the different parts of government. He also mentioned the widening rift between North and South over the issue of slavery, promising that he would not try to end slavery in any state. Finally, Harrison told the crowd that he would not seek a second term. The inaugural address lasted for more than an hour and a half, making it the longest in U.S. history. This speech is one of the few clues historians have to help them guess what Harrison might have done had he completed his term in office. The address, given in such frigid weather, could also have contributed to his coming down with a cold.

◀ Harrison being
sworn into office
before giving the
longest inaugural
address in
U.S. history

Once in the White House, President Harrison found himself surrounded by people looking for jobs. Meanwhile, his relations with Henry Clay only got worse. The senator believed that Harrison was ignoring his advice. Their quarrels grew until Clay angrily left Washington on March 15.

Harrison took his job seriously. During March, he visited each government department, eager to see how things worked. He wanted government employees who did good work to keep their jobs, whether they were Democrats or Whigs. This made many Whigs mad. They wanted to punish Democrats by removing as many of them as possible from office.

George E. Badger ▾ served as secretary of the navy in Harrison's cabinet. Harrison sometimes clashed with his advisers over how much power they should have in making decisions that would affect the nation.

Harrison also clashed with his Whig cabinet members, who thought that all decisions should be left to them. In fact, they believed that each cabinet member—including Harrison—should have one vote in all matters. They thought that the president should be the "first among equals"—meaning that he should be nothing more than the person running the cabinet meetings. Harrison, however, didn't always agree with this.

After taking office, Harrison remained easygoing. He often walked around the city and sometimes even did the shopping for the White House kitchen. During one walk, Harrison was caught in a downpour and came down with another cold. On March 27, the cold worsened. Doctors said the president had a lung disease called pneumonia.

A number of doctors were called in to treat the president. They tried the most popular cures of the day, but these were often worse than the disease. The doctors put heated suction cups on the president's body to draw out the illness. They tried "bleeding" him, which involved cutting a vein to drain what they believed was bad blood. The doctors even tried Native American cures, but they had little success.

▲ One attempted cure for illness in the 1800s was "bleeding," which involved drawing blood out of a patient's vein.

President William Henry Harrison died just after midnight on April 4, 1841. He had served as president for exactly one month.

As his body lay in the Capitol, the nation grieved. Newspapers outlined columns in black, and black **crepe** hung everywhere. Harrison was buried in Washington, D.C., on April 7, 1841. In June, his remains were reburied in North Bend, Ohio.

Harrison on his deathbed in April 1841

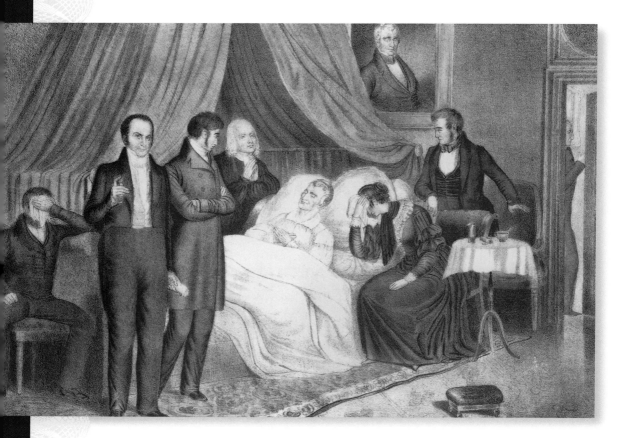

The president's death sent Washington into a turmoil. Harrison was the first president to die while in office. No one was sure what to do. Vice President John Tyler was next in line to be president, but how would he handle his new role? Would he simply serve as the acting president and call for new presidential elections, or would he let Congress choose a new president? Tyler did neither. He had himself sworn in as president and made Congress aware that he intended to serve out Harrison's term. Tyler quickly made many political enemies. He became known as His Accidency, and his presidency forced Congress to more clearly outline how power should be transferred when a president dies. It also encouraged Americans to look more carefully at the vice presidential candidate as a person who might one day serve as the leader of the nation.

▲ *John Tyler became president after Harrison's death.*

During Harrison's short time in office, he proved that he was not ready to blindly bend to Henry Clay's wishes or the decisions of his Whig cabinet members. Although he was not president for very long, he took his duties to the nation seriously. There is no question that Harrison intended to do what was best for the country he had served so loyally throughout his life.

Harrison took his ▶ position seriously during his short time in office.

GLOSSARY

★ ★ ★

cabinet—a president's group of advisers who are heads of government departments

campaign—an organized effort to win an election

candidates—people running for office in an election

Constitution—the document stating the basic laws of the United States

convention—a large meeting during which a political party chooses its candidates

crepe—a delicate crinkled material

depression—a time when businesses do badly and many people become poor

minister—an official who represents one country in another country

puppet—a person who does, says, and thinks what another orders

slogan—a phrase used to capture public attention in a campaign

strategy—a careful plan

WILLIAM HENRY HARRISON'S LIFE AT A GLANCE

★ ★ ★

PERSONAL

Nickname: Old Tippecanoe, Old Tip

Born: February 9, 1773

Birthplace: Charles City County, Virginia

Father's name: Benjamin Harrison

Mother's name: Elizabeth Bassett Harrison

Education: Attended Hampden-Sydney College

Wife's name: Anna Tuthill Symmes (1775–1864)

Married: November 25, 1795

Children: Elizabeth Bassett Harrison (1796–1846); John Cleves Symmes Harrison (1798–1830); Lucy Singleton Harrison (1800–1826); William Henry Harrison (1802–1838); John Scott Harrison (1804–1878); Benjamin Harrison (1806–1840); Mary Symmes Harrison (1809–1842); Carter Bassett Harrison (1811–1839); Anna Tuthill Harrison (1813–1865); James Findlay Harrison (1814–1817)

Died: April 4, 1841, in Washington, D.C.

Buried: William Henry Harrison Memorial State Park, North Bend, Ohio

PUBLIC

Occupation before presidency: Soldier, politician

Occupation after presidency: None

Military service: Army officer who defeated Native Americans at the Battle of Tippecanoe in 1811; major general in command of the Army of the Northwest during the War of 1812

Other government positions: Secretary of Northwest Territory; territorial delegate to U.S. Congress; governor of the Indiana Territory; U.S. representative from Ohio; Ohio state senator; U.S. senator from Ohio; minister to Colombia

Political party: Whig

Vice president: John Tyler (1841)

Dates in office: March 4, 1841–April 4, 1841

Presidential opponents: Daniel Webster (Whig) and Hugh Lawson White (Whig), 1836; Martin Van Buren (Democrat), 1836 and 1840

Number of votes (Electoral College): 549,508 of 1,501,630 (73 of 294), 1836; 1,274,624 of 2,402,405 (234 of 294), 1840

Writings: None

William Henry Harrison's Cabinet

Secretary of state:
  Daniel Webster (1841)

Secretary of the treasury:
  Thomas Ewing (1841)

Secretary of war:
  John Bell (1841)

Attorney general:
  John J. Crittenden (1841)

Postmaster general:
  Francis Granger (1841)

Secretary of the navy:
  George E. Badger (1841)

WILLIAM HENRY HARRISON'S LIFE AND TIMES

★ ★ ★

HARRISON'S LIFE		WORLD EVENTS
February 9, Harrison is born in Charles City County, Virginia	1773	

		1777	Vermont is the first former colony to ban slavery
		1779	Jan Ingenhousz of the Netherlands discovers that plants release oxygen when exposed to sunlight

1780

		1783	American author Washington Irving is born

Enters Hampden-Sydney College	1785		
Travels to Philadelphia to study medicine	1790		

1790

Father dies	1791	1791	Austrian composer Wolfgang Amadeus Mozart (above) dies
Joins the U.S. Army			

HARRISON'S LIFE		WORLD EVENTS	
Serves under General Anthony Wayne (below)	1792–1794	1792	The dollar currency is introduced to America

		1793	King Louis XVI of France is executed
		1794	The U.S. Navy is established
Becomes commander of Fort Washington (below)	1795		

Marries Anna Tuthill Symmes			

Leaves the army	1798		
Appointed secretary of the Northwest Territory		1799	Napoléon Bonaparte (above) takes control of France
			The Rosetta Stone, which was the key to understanding Egyptian hieroglyphics, is found near Rosetta, Egypt

HARRISON'S LIFE

Becomes territorial 1800
representative

Appointed governor of
the Indiana Territory

Defeats Native American 1811
forces at the Battle
of Tippecanoe (above)

Named commander of the 1812
Army of the Northwest

1800

1810

WORLD EVENTS

1801   Ultraviolet radiation
is discovered

1807   Robert Fulton's *Clermont*
(below) is the first reliable
steamship to travel
between New York
City and Albany

1809   American poet and short-
story writer Edgar Allen
Poe is born in Boston

1810   Bernardo O'Higgins
leads Chile in its fight for
independence from Spain

1812–   The United States and
1814   Britain fight the War
of 1812 (below)

HARRISON'S LIFE

Defeats British and **1813**
Native American forces
at the Battle of the
Thames (below) during
the War of 1812

Serves in the **1816–**
U.S. House of **1819**
Representatives

Serves as Ohio **1819–**
state senator **1821**

Runs for governor of **1820**
Ohio but loses

Runs for the U.S. House **1822**
of Representatives
but loses

Wins a seat as a U.S. **1825**
senator from Ohio

WORLD EVENTS

1814– European states meet in
1815 Vienna, Austria, to redraw
national borders after the
conclusion of the
Napoleonic Wars

1820 Susan B. Anthony (above),
a leader of the American
woman suffrage
movement, is born

1821 Central American
countries gain
independence from Spain

1823 Mexico becomes
a republic

1826 The first photograph is
taken by Joseph Niépce,
a French physicist

1820

HARRISON'S LIFE

WORLD EVENTS

1827   Modern-day matches are invented by coating the end of a wooden stick with phosphorus

Becomes U.S.   1828
minister to Colombia

1829   The first practical sewing machine is invented by French tailor Barthélemy Thimonnier (above)

1830

1833   Great Britain abolishes slavery

Runs as one of three   1836
Whig candidates for
president but loses
to Democrat Martin
Van Buren (above)

1836   Texans defeat Mexican troops at San Jacinto after a deadly battle at the Alamo (below)

HARRISON'S LIFE

WORLD EVENTS

1837   American banker
J. P. Morgan is born

1840

Presidential Election Results:	Popular Votes	Electoral Votes
1840 William Henry Harrison	1,274,624	234
Martin Van Buren	1,127,781	60

1840   Auguste Rodin, famous
sculptor of *The Thinker*
(below), is born

March 4, sworn in as   1841
the ninth U.S.
president; gives the
longest inaugural
address in U.S. history

March 27, health
worsens after he
catches a cold that
develops into
pneumonia

April 4, dies after just
one month in office

1843   One thousand pioneers
head west from Indepen-
dence, Missouri, and
travel along the Oregon
Trail in an event that
becomes known as the
Great Migration

UNDERSTANDING WILLIAM HENRY HARRISON AND HIS PRESIDENCY

★ ★ ★

IN THE LIBRARY

Gaines, Ann Graham. *William Henry Harrison: Our Ninth President.*
Chanhassen, Minn.: The Child's World, 2002.

Otfinoski, Steven. *William Henry Harrison.* New York:
Children's Press, 2003.

Stefoff, Rebecca. *Tecumseh and the Shawnee Confederation.*
New York: Facts on File, 1998.

ON THE WEB

The White House—William Henry Harrison
http://www.whitehouse.gov/history/presidents/wh9.html
For a short biography of Harrison

Internet Public Library—William Henry Harrison
http://www.ipl.org/div/potus/whharrison.html
For information about Harrison's presidency
and many links to other resources

The American President—William Henry Harrison
http://www.americanpresident.org/history/williamhharrison
For in-depth information about Harrison

HARRISON HISTORIC SITES
ACROSS THE COUNTRY

Grouseland
3 West Scott Street
Vincennes, Indiana 47591
812/882-2096
To visit the home where
Harrison lived while he was
governor of Indiana Territory

**William Henry Harrison
Memorial State Park**
Cliff Road & U.S. Highway 50
North Bend, Ohio 45052
614/297-2630
To see the tombs of Anna and
William Henry Harrison

Tippecanoe Battlefield
Battle Ground, Indiana 47901
317/567-2147
To visit a monument and
museum related to the Battle
of Tippecanoe

Berkeley Hundred Plantation
12602 Harrison Landing Road
Charles City, Virginia 23030
804/829-6018
To visit the home where
Harrison was born

THE U.S. PRESIDENTS
(Years in Office)

★ ★ ★

1. **George Washington**
   (March 4, 1789–March 3, 1797)
2. **John Adams**
   (March 4, 1797–March 3, 1801)
3. **Thomas Jefferson**
   (March 4, 1801–March 3, 1809)
4. **James Madison**
   (March 4, 1809–March 3, 1817)
5. **James Monroe**
   (March 4, 1817–March 3, 1825)
6. **John Quincy Adams**
   (March 4, 1825–March 3, 1829)
7. **Andrew Jackson**
   (March 4, 1829–March 3, 1837)
8. **Martin Van Buren**
   (March 4, 1837–March 3, 1841)
9. **William Henry Harrison**
   (March 6, 1841–April 4, 1841)
10. **John Tyler**
    (April 6, 1841–March 3, 1845)
11. **James K. Polk**
    (March 4, 1845–March 3, 1849)
12. **Zachary Taylor**
    (March 5, 1849–July 9, 1850)
13. **Millard Fillmore**
    (July 10, 1850–March 3, 1853)
14. **Franklin Pierce**
    (March 4, 1853–March 3, 1857)
15. **James Buchanan**
    (March 4, 1857–March 3, 1861)
16. **Abraham Lincoln**
    (March 4, 1861–April 15, 1865)
17. **Andrew Johnson**
    (April 15, 1865–March 3, 1869)

18. **Ulysses S. Grant**
    (March 4, 1869–March 3, 1877)
19. **Rutherford B. Hayes**
    (March 4, 1877–March 3, 1881)
20. **James Garfield**
    (March 4, 1881–Sept 19, 1881)
21. **Chester Arthur**
    (Sept 20, 1881–March 3, 1885)
22. **Grover Cleveland**
    (March 4, 1885–March 3, 1889)
23. **Benjamin Harrison**
    (March 4, 1889–March 3, 1893)
24. **Grover Cleveland**
    (March 4, 1893–March 3, 1897)
25. **William McKinley**
    (March 4, 1897–
    September 14, 1901)
26. **Theodore Roosevelt**
    (September 14, 1901–
    March 3, 1909)
27. **William Howard Taft**
    (March 4, 1909–March 3, 1913)
28. **Woodrow Wilson**
    (March 4, 1913–March 3, 1921)
29. **Warren G. Harding**
    (March 4, 1921–August 2, 1923)
30. **Calvin Coolidge**
    (August 3, 1923–March 3, 1929)
31. **Herbert Hoover**
    (March 4, 1929–March 3, 1933)
32. **Franklin D. Roosevelt**
    (March 4, 1933–April 12, 1945)

33. **Harry S. Truman**
    (April 12, 1945–
    January 20, 1953)
34. **Dwight D. Eisenhower**
    (January 20, 1953–
    January 20, 1961)
35. **John F. Kennedy**
    (January 20, 1961–
    November 22, 1963)
36. **Lyndon B. Johnson**
    (November 22, 1963–
    January 20, 1969)
37. **Richard M. Nixon**
    (January 20, 1969–
    August 9, 1974)
38. **Gerald R. Ford**
    (August 9, 1974–
    January 20, 1977)
39. **James Earl Carter**
    (January 20, 1977–
    January 20, 1981)
40. **Ronald Reagan**
    (January 20, 1981–
    January 20, 1989)
41. **George H. W. Bush**
    (January 20, 1989–
    January 20, 1993)
42. **William Jefferson Clinton**
    (January 20, 1993–
    January 20, 2001)
43. **George W. Bush**
    (January 20, 2001–)

INDEX

★ ★ ★

Index

ABOUT THE AUTHOR

Robin S. Doak has been writing for children for more than fourteen years. A former editor of *Weekly Reader* and *U*S*Kids* magazine, Ms. Doak has authored fun and educational materials for kids of all ages. Some of her work includes biographies of explorers such as Henry Hudson and John Smith, as well as other titles in this series. Ms. Doak is a past winner of an Educational Press Association of America Distinguished Achievement Award. She lives with her husband and three children in central Connecticut.